etymology of the
soul

Harriet Austin

Presentation by *BookLeaf Publishing*

Web: www.bookleafpub.com

E-mail: info@bookleafpub.com

ISBN: 9789358313499

First edition 2023

*To my family, to myself, and to those who
are trying to find your place in this world. I
hope you might find something here.*

ACKNOWLEDGEMENT

I'd firstly like to thank my mum, for letting me pitch half-written poems to her late at night when she was trying to sleep. (Seriously, I think she wanted to go to bed.) I'd like to thank my brothers, my sister, and the rest of my family for their support on my first official publication.
A special thank you to BookLeafPublishing who have allowed me and so many other aspiring authors to achieve their publication dreams. Thanks guys!
And finally, to Dan Rowley and Tristan Simpson, who are just about the best English teachers I've ever had the honour of being a student of.

midnight interlude

under a venetian sky
she lay on the paved street,
bricks cool against her back
she watched the rainpour smother the ground
and the white light of the moon
reflected, shimmering, in the water
until the street was full of stars

an empty room
with plain and towering walls -
he sat against the door,
eyes facing the ceiling
and realised he could write a poem
for every crack in the wall,
every crease in the curtain,
every coffee stain

they meet in another life, maybe
both students in Chem,
or baristas in the same corner café on the high
street,
but for now
one lay in a sea of stars,
and the other in a room with mocha-stained
walls,

through the starry water, she hears him speak -
"since when did it hurt? since when was the
weight of the world so vast? It hurts to breathe,
to live - how do I survive when what is human
becomes painful?"
through the deepening cracks in the wall, he
hears her reply.

they don't meet in this life.
their dreams drift past one another in a breeze,
brushing fingertips, nearly touching.
their words echo in the same wells, between the
same bricks.
their eyes shine in the night sky, their flaws in
the cracks on empty walls.

ragtime beat

dawn breaks, like bones
and rifle-ends peek over the sand bags.
watching eyes; tiny voids
holding a man's life within the diameter
a commander's cold call -
and the boys, young boys,
too tall for their trousers and
too lanky for a gun -
bolt. over the sandbags.
shoelaces caught in the sharp blackthorn,
bullets caught in juvenile hearts,
shrapnel caught in ankles when they stumble
through the churned land
a doleful memory in the backs of their minds of
something green,
and vibrant. Alive.

he curls into the crevice of a crater, back pressed
against ashy soil,
clutching his gaping leg,
blood leaking, ivory bone peaking from the
opening.
behind him,
ammunition spurts from the barrels -
beating on the ground like ragtime:

duple meter, steady bass, treble lead.

the sun floats above the horizon line
she watches, and she waits -
an apathetic negligence
to the blood spilled beneath her
golden light

Ra-tat. Ra-tat. Ra-tat. Ragtime beat.

soon,
the sky is black. the blood is still crimson -
skin attatches to skin in a web;
a face becomes pasty and pale.
his helmet, a steel drum over his heart,
juvenile.
an explosion, bomb, bullet -
no.
a bursting flare from his side of the battle
illuminates the sky for a second. one.
second.
the flare - a single candle, waxy and small,
in the corner of a room
black with neglect.
the flare, it's own sun, that burns as brightly
and shines as stubbornly.
fireworks.

when the other lads stumble to this night's

home,
stretcher on their backs,
(they've lost one of 'em on the way here.)
in his diamond-clear eyes,
they catch a glimpse of the sun
and watch as on his burst-open leg
he taps:
ra-tat, ra-tat, a ragtime beat.

women of the tempest

eight shadows
linger in the waves
- echoless, soundless screams
resonate in only the white foam
that coats the tumbling waters

Bellamy strolls along the beach
just out of the water
tearing up pages of the divine
letting them dissolve in the ocean
as the sea grasps for her skin
but she turns her back to the raging water

Helena basks in the salt
red silk floating around her hips
holding a white camellias in her hands
she casts each petal into the
darkening, willing ocean
and waits, as the waves wash over her head

Colette wanders into the sea
with half a locket clutched in her hand
and a half full bottle of champagne
in the other
she feeds it to the gluttonous depths,

and it devours each drop

Ophelia tugs at the necklace
around her neck - mother of pearl.
she sits by the rocks
pulling the necklace apart,
and throws each spherical stone into the waters
which, giggling, grab at the pearls with joy

Elisabeth screams in rage
(there is something about her anger
that feels suited to a woman - feminine.
unchained.)
she yells at the waves and shouts
at the tide. the tide that
holds less mercy than she

Genevieve lays beneath the stormy sky
and wonders
why the others despise it so.
the salt that washes over her skin
feels kind and gentle. she doesn't mind.
she forgets. she forgets that the salt is not as kind
as she.

Violet has blood on her hands
she strides with sorrowful purpose into the
roaring waves.

the stones and shells beneath her cut into her
skin
but she walks.
and walks.
and walks.

Elodie smiles and toys with the bracelet
that encircles her wrist.
with a grin, she unties it
and hurls it into the sand
for the tide to wash away.
the tide pretends to turn away. the tide will wash
her away too.

Claudine stands by Bellamy.
"who needs that book anyway? if He's
abandoned
you, abandon Him."

she hovers by Helena.
"let it take you. let it wash over you. you'll feel
better."

she waits on the beach for Colette.
"feed it the drink. it is more hungry than you."

she sits by Ophelia.

"pearls are worthless to you. throw it away. the
water will treasure them."

she holds Elisabeth's arm as she screams.
"it did this to you. to him. it deserves your fury.
make it pay."

she lays by Genevieve.
"you think differently. I like it."

she watches as Violet goes out further.
"keep going. there is nothing left for you."

she rests her head on Elodie's shoulder.
"i didn't love mine, either. it was all
play-pretend. we all lie sometimes."

the shadows in the depths call out.
sixteen distorted voices ring in the waves.
they fizz with dissolving paper
the foam is white with flower petals
and bubbles with champagne
pearly light reflects on the surface
the waves roar, they scream
people know why the women despise it so
the blood that washes on the shore is crimson.

claudine watches as a young man wanders to the
beach.

he has tears streaked down his pale skin.
"are you alright?" she asks.
"it is my wife. her name is Bellamy. she is
dead."
"oh," she says. "come to the water. the ocean is
kind."

graveyard shift

i am alive in only a single sense of the word -
physically, for I am breathing.
inside, is a graveyard, where bones are buried in
the earth and headstones drown in moss and rain
and the poetry flows like water,
feeding my soul with whiskey and wine.
and it feels like a Hell that warms my heart,
caged in my ribs with shackles of bone;
my soul is intoxicated with the euphoria of
verses and lines, it drunkens me, leaving me
drowsy and breathless.
the confusion is almost revitalising, nearly
rasing me from the graveyard
but it doesn't.
a bittersweet delusion - that i will stop decaying
in my coffin
when the words rush through me like coldness
striking my nerves,
and the verses spill onto the page.
i want it to revive me, but really, it doesn't.
for i write and write until my hands go numb at
midnight,
but i still lie on the memory foam mattress on
my bed
and the ceiling is still blank,

and the headstones read my name - all of my
names
the girl i was when i was five,
the girl I'll be in three years,
the girl I was yesterday, and who I'll be
tomorrow.

the ceiling is blank.

i look at the clock, and two minutes have
passed, and i still can't tell if I'm alive or not.

she bleeds in calligraphy and ink

she lies on the tiled ground
shuddering in pain

thick, black ink streams down her pale skin
from slices in her arms and legs

it is the colour of
a crow's feather in the moonlight
a glistening, onyx piano key
a petal of a black rose coated in dew

empty notebooks across the floor
begin to fill with words -

intricate calligraphy pours from her wounds
curling and flicking each letter

with the passion of
a thousand heartbreaks
a thousand betrayals
a thousand emotions

she can feel each line of a poem
being pumped through her veins

by an ebony heart

each word flowing behind her eyes
until every expression
every syllable and phrase
blooms on the paper from the slashes on her
body

like a flower in a battlefield

dark nightingale

pasty, pale -
she has charcoal hair and swan-white skin.
you'll find her in the midst of a battlefield
when she stands on the sidelines and
she
waits.

for the bullet to deflect from the armour
and to strike a boy in the chest:

she moves swiftly - a quiet and stealthy
nightingale -
between the swinging axes and firing rifles
to hover over his body, and take her gold:

his eyes fall still, and his body drops to the earth.

"I am with you," she whispers. "I remain."

her voice echoes softly in the ears of the falling;
a blood curdling cacophony in
those who stand.

you'll find her at funerals,

loitering in the back left corner,
a dark veil sheathing her eyes

she speaks, slowly, to empty air
disordered sounds from between blood-reddened
lips
that,
when nobody remains in the darkening room,
only the corpse in the coffin can hear -

"Death is with you. Death remains."

aurora borealis

you let down your hair
and I waver in your grasp
some angel of death,
come to take my soul and leave me
withered, decaying
lifeless, soulless
you want to take me to paradise,
at least, you tell me so
but no god made a better paradise
than whatever hell we live in, love
it's tortorous, and it's ours
the glimmer of your gauntlets, breastplate
light the sky with a haze
- teal, green, purple.
and we're young again. but
warriors bleed and souls wither away
so you pull me to heaven
and the feathers glisten
in the sky
like the ocean's heavy waves,
it's daunting reflection.

icarus

when he lept from the ledge,
they called him reckless.
when he danced beneath the sun -
bronze feathers catching the light -
they called him careless.
when he stretched his hands
towards the golden brilliance, towards
Apollo's throne, and warmth
they called him thoughtless.
when he fell,
they said he should have known.

how could he?

how could he have cared -
a boy, drunk on sunlight and
salty air,
fire and wax in his lungs -

when he grazed Apollo's hands,
felt his breath, felt his Kingdom

first law

sloping down, an arc of smooth stone -
and soon, the curve meets my skin,
the curve of Earth and her
Venus.
no friction burns; no resistance.
constant movement.
the level ground lasts for hours
and I wonder if I am closer to God
or a dog - falling so easily,
infinite distance, neverending.
all I know is I am not human,
in my marble form: spherical
and dense.
this patience takes desperation.
I will never meet your hand at the
upward arc - the mountain climb -
and you will let me wane
until I am dust

Earnshaw

half-a-soul, sin-seeker
venom on your tongue, violent
heart, bound with bone;
nature's own confinement
of a love that shouldn't exist.
veins and arteries snare around your ankles,
chains to hold you down.
your love is a bloody rebellion,
your heart the weapon,
the anger of a people.
your love can shake monarchies,
burn kingdoms to charcoal,
so you love in the ashes and soot.

the slaughterhouse

welcome to the slaughterhouse
our stained windows are crimson with blood
bring me your lambs, sheep and goats
lay them beside the altar
let the blinding light of the sun
form halos around their mangled faces
and disguise the red blotches in their fur.
the butcher is waiting -
his robes as white as a pearl
but his hands are scarlet
as a ruby
glistening in a fire.

the same red
as yours

the sunlight glowing before you casts
a shadow so deep that
if you look at a certain angle,
palms faced towards the golden light
it seems as though your hands are
almost clean.

grecian temples and orange peel

marble sculptures
and splintering columns
heaven bleeding through gaps between stone
and casting golden light
onto the strong jaw of Athena

you wait for me by the pillars
orange on your lips and in melting hues
within your eyes.
you braid a marigold in my hair
(because you say it suits me, or something)
and you hand me
the rest of your orange -

as i sit on the steps beneath the sunset and
tear into the fruit,
it occurs to me that i see you -
warm and orange and fiery -
in the sun when it sinks into the horizon's loving
embrace
and in the marigolds
that encompass foreign fields with an amber
haze

the waters that divide us

the asphodel meadows are often bleak,
souls aimlessly wander
"my regrets will follow you to the grave" -
well, they have followed for sure
chased and hunted and tracked
tangling me in a web of sorrow and guilt
chaining me to the ground
and pulling me under -
as if burying me alive

you've never had that problem, angel
but asphodels are eternal
like guilt
like you

I watch you from my side of the water -
Mnemosyne -
you glow beneath no light
there is life in your face, your features
like you have been caressed
with persephone's tender kiss
lillies bloom on your skin
your hair is wisteria, flowing in a breeze
and a cluster of camellias sheath your heart

and I watch,
on my side of the waters,
and wonder, in my desolate field of asphodels,
if you, in your paradise
Elysium
watch me and think of me too

a crown of leaves

the sunrise illuminates
a crown of leaves and moss
that rests upon her brow

the green holds her
closely and dearly
in the depths of a dimly lit forest
in the early mornings of spring

her skin
is pasty and cold and bruised
but flowers bloom on the ground beneath it
and curl up her arms
like vines
shaping teardrops, crosses
upon flesh once rich and brown

tree roots
embrace her
and anchor her
to the soft and light ground
sheathing her figure
as if she were a precious, jewelled blade
and they were it's blacksmith,
her creator

no one visits
no one weeps

none but the trees that sway and mourn
in the bitter evening wind
none but the flowers, whose heads droop
as the sun sets
and the moon rises
again

seclusion

to be alone
is to be in an empty room
hands pressed against cold glass
to gaze in furious envy at the laughing,
grinning, saccharine smiles
vibrant faces, radiating a sugar-sweet air
so sickly that it can almost be tasted on the glass
to be alone
is to notice the expanse
between your feet and the wall
to feel the cold, deserted air biting in its jest
bitter and piercing
the echo of your heartbeat against the grey
concrete blocks
makes a sound more prominent than laughter

signed, Little Red

the glass that hurt you, Mr Wolf,
rests in your palms
the words that struck your heart like a blade, Mr
Wolf,
drip in acid from your tongue.

the world that made you suffer, Mr Wolf,
weeps in a melancholy echo
that lingers
when the night falls silent.

it weeps, Mr Wolf,
from your rage.

your fangs are beared, Mr Wolf,
were they inherited? or did you create them?
your eyes are feral, Mr Wolf.
is the pain a disease? caught?

I feel sorry for you, Mr Wolf,
even though you want me dead.

you tried so hard
to escape your monster
that you became one, instead.

your hands

I hold your hands in mine at midnight,
souls intertwined, and fingers
I scribble flowers and words
onto yourporcelain skin
shakespeare on your wrists
blue ink on white palms -
flames licking the marbled walls
of a palace
the charcoal stains,
a reminder of my love
that fades
with the arrival of dawn

are we angels?

Are we angels?

do our wings glisten in the shining sun?
the halos of light encircling our graceful heads -
do they glow as brightly as we want them to?
the harmonious chorus of our voices;
is the echo as ethereal as the wind in a field of
lavender,
on a bright, spring day?
it's unlikely.
the plump faces of cherubs are fed by greed,
and pair upon pairs of malicious eyes
observe each person,
each conversation,
each action performed.
our divine cacophony is distorted and dissonant
behind the harps that play in the clouds,
our halos burn hot with searing and painful light,
our wings do not glisten in the sun
but in the flames
of Hell.

We are not angels.
We have never been.